Text: Jayna Maleri
Jacket/Interior Design: Kimberly Adis
Interior Layout: Kimberly Shake
Cover Photographer: Alexandra Grablewski
Executive Editor, Series: Shawna Mullen
Assistant Editor, Series: Timothy Stobierski
Series Art Director: Rosalind Loeb Wanke
Series Production Editor: Lynne Phillips
Copy Editor: Candace B. Levy

The Taunton Press
Inspiration for hands-on living®

The Taunton Press, Inc., 63 South Main Street,
PO Box 5506, Newtown, CT 06470-5506
e-mail: tp@taunton.com

Threads® is a trademark of The Taunton Press, Inc.,
registered in the U.S. Patent and Trademark Office.

The following names/manufacturers appearing in
Super Cute Duct Tape are trademarks: Duck®,
Duck Fabric®, Duck Washi®, Etsy™, Walmart®

Library of Congress Cataloging-in-Publication Data in
progress
ISBN 978-1-62710-990-1

Printed in the United States of America
10 9 8 7 6 5 4 3 2 1

contents

tape it!

Clear, duct, double-stick—tape comes in all shapes, sizes, and strengths. But the newest member of the tape family might be its most adorable yet. Yes, I'm stuck on fabric tape. Available in a variety of vibrant patterns—from classics like gingham and pinstripes to abstract wave prints and free-form polka dots—fabric tape adds color and texture to any project. And whether you choose to embellish a pair of sneakers or to create a bouquet of blooms that will last forever, using fabric tape couldn't be simpler: Just cut, peel, stick, and go!

Fabric tape is not machine washable, so be sure to keep that in mind when embellishing clothing or accessories. I recommend spot cleaning such pieces, or removing the tape before washing.

Ready? Set? Start sticking!

types of tape

The projects in this book use a variety of fabric tapes as well as a few additional styles. Here, you'll find a quick rundown of what they are.

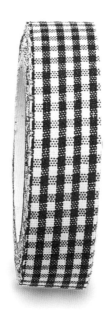

FABRIC TAPE

The star of the show, you can find fabric tape at craft and hobby stores and online. I used Duck® brand Duck Fabric® crafting tape, which comes in rolls of two widths, as well as 8 in. by 10. in. sheets. The tapes come with paper backing, which allows you to perfectly trim and place each strip before committing to sticking. Maya Road also offers a wide variety of fabric tapes you can use.

WASHI TAPE

Not made of fabric, washi tape is easy to tear, is a cinch to reposition, and is available in hundreds of colors, patterns, and prints. It's ideal for just about any craft project that involves tape. For the projects in this book, I used a variety of Duck Washi® crafting tapes.

LACE TAPE

For any project that calls for a bit of texture, turn to lace tape. Paper-backed like fabric tape, it adds polish and depth to pillows, curtains, totes, and more. I used it as an accent on the Pretty-in-Pink Foldover Clutch (p. 11), and to brighten up a simple leather belt (p. 7).

The Sweetest Sneakers

Talk about all-stars: A few fabric tape accents transform hot pink high-tops into a charming and completely personalized pair.

SKILL LEVEL

Intermediate

MATERIALS

Fabric crafting tape of your choice

Scissors

High-top sneakers

Chalk

TO MAKE THE SNEAKERS

1. Cut a strip of tape large enough to cover the toe of your sneaker. Remove the paper backing from the tape strip and place it on the toe, smoothing into place.

2. Use chalk to trace the toe of your sneaker on the tape strip. Remove the tape strip from the sneaker and cut along the traced line. Place this cutout on your sneaker toe and smooth into place.

3. Cut a small shape (heart, star, flower, peace sign, and so on) out of tape. Remove the paper backing and place the tape shape near the ankle of the shoe. Cut a small strip of tape to cover each shoelace end.

4. Measure the back seam of the sneaker and cut a strip of tape wide enough to cover it. Remove the paper backing and run the strip of tape up the back seam, smoothing into place as you go. Repeat the entire process with the second sneaker.

> **TIP** I used a complementary shade of pink on my sneakers, but don't be afraid to experiment with different color combinations, like pink and turquoise, pink and red, or pink and black!

Build-a-Belt

This bold, striped accessory (**A**) is the perfect finishing touch to wear with your favorite pair of boyfriend jeans.

SKILL LEVEL
Intermediate

MATERIALS
Cloth measuring tape
Fabric crafting tape of your choice
Scissors
2 metal D-rings

TO MAKE THE BELT

1. To determine how long your belt should be, use the measuring tape to measure your waist, add 3 in., and cut a length of tape to fit that measurement. Remove the paper backing from the tape strip and lay it on your work surface, sticky-side up.

2. Fold the tape strip lengthwise. Start by folding one side in toward the center of the strip, then repeat with the second side. You should end up with no visible sticky side.

3. Once the sticky side has been covered, create stripes by cutting skinnier lengths of complementary tape and placing them on the original length of tape. When you are happy with your design, string the D-rings onto the tape at one end.

4. Fold the tape strip over itself and over the D-rings, then secure the rings in the loop created by the folded-over tape by winding another piece of tape around the belt. Trim the opposite end of the belt into a rounded shape, if desired.

VARIATION To dress-up a leather belt in five seconds flat (**B**), cut a length of lace tape, remove the paper backing and run it down the center of the belt. You can add a few dots of strong glue to help the tape stay in place if necessary.

Vibrant Valance

Pair this tape-embellished valance with your favorite patterned curtains or let your craft take center stage by matching it to a solid-colored shade.

SKILL LEVEL
Beginner

MATERIALS
Cloth measuring tape
Chalk
Valance
Fabric crafting tape of your choice
Scissors

TO MAKE THE VALANCE

1. Working with your valance on a flat surface, use the measuring tape and chalk to measure and mark a few inches in from the top left hand corner of the valance.

2. Using the chalk mark you just created as your starting point, measure diagonally toward the bottom of the valance, stopping a few inches above the bottom edge. Add 1 in. to this measurement and use it as your guide to cut 10 to 12 strips of tape (depending on the length of the valance).

3. Remove the paper backing from one strip of tape and place it on the

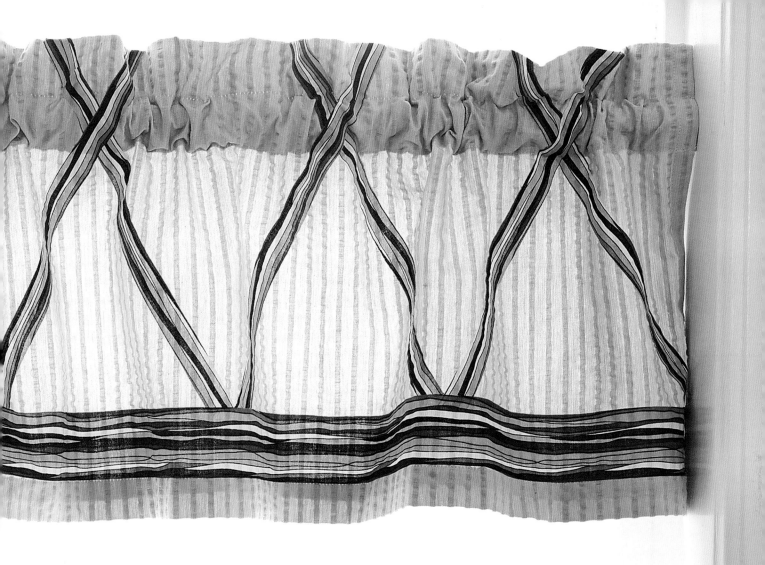

valance, starting at the chalk mark and moving diagonally downward to the right. Fold the excess 1 in. of tape over the top edge of the valance, securing in place in back.

4. Remove the paper backing from the second strip of tape and place it on the valance, starting 2 in. to 3 in. farther in from the top end of your first piece and folding the excess tape over the top edge of the valance. Moving diagonally downward and to the left, place the tape on the valance. The second strip of tape will cross over the first, creating a tepee shape when you are finished.

5. Continue in this way, placing strips of tape in crisscrossing shapes until the entire length of the valance is covered, making sure the pattern is even as you go.

6. To finish the valance, cut a piece of tape that is 2 in. longer than the length of the valance. Remove the paper backing and place the strip along the bottom edge, covering the edges of each tepee as you go. Fold the excess tape over the left and right edges of the valance.

TIP Once you've created one tepee shape, measure its size and use that as your guide to map out the rest of the valance. Do this before removing the paper backing and sticking the tape to the fabric. If you realize the shape is too wide or narrow to repeat evenly over the entire valance, adjust the tape until you have a tepee shape that works.

Dressed-Up Picture Frames

A few strips of tape are a quick, easy, and inexpensive way to give your old picture frames a modern look.

SKILL LEVEL

Beginner

MATERIALS

Picture frame (wood frames work best)

Cloth measuring tape

Fabric crafting tape of your choice

Scissors

TO MAKE THE PICTURE FRAME

1. Measure the area of the frame that you want to cover. Cut strips of tape to fit these measurements. You can angle the ends of each strip so that they fit together snugly in the corners or leave them straight for a layered look.

2. Remove the paper backing from the tape strip and place the tape on the frame, smoothing into place.

3. Repeat with the remaining frames.

TIP Get creative with your frames! I used striped and gingham tape on one, spotted tape on another, and a combination of tape and adhesive-backed fabric sheets in different colors and patterns on the third.

Pretty-in-Pink Foldover Clutch

There are lots of things to love about this adorable accessory, but my favorite has to be the fact that it's made from a plastic storage bag!

SKILL LEVEL
Intermediate

MATERIALS
1 gallon-size plastic storage bag
Fabric crafting tape of your choice
Scissors
Lace tape of your choice

TO MAKE THE CLUTCH

1. Place the plastic bag on a flat surface (you may find it easier to work with the bag taped down at the top and bottom to prevent sliding). Cut strips of fabric tape longer than the width of your bag (about 1 in. longer works best).

2. Working with one strip at a time, remove the paper backing from the tape and place it on the bag from left to right. The 1-in. overage will stick to your flat surface, which is OK.

3. Continue placing strips of fabric tape on your bag, overlapping slightly as you go, until one side of the bag is entirely covered. Carefully peel the bag off of the flat surface and trim the overhanging tape.

4. Flip the bag over and repeat on the second side. To finish the edges apply strips of matching tape to the sides and bottom of the bag.

5. Embellish your clutch as desired. I used lace tape to give it a textural, three-dimensional design.

TIP Once the tape makes contact with your storage bag, it's difficult to get it unstuck, so work slowly and carefully to ensure each strip is placed exactly where you want it to go.

Upcycled Vases

Don't toss those old glass bottles! Give them a rinse, allow them to dry completely, and then turn them into these utterly sweet DIY vases (**A**).

SKILL LEVEL
Intermediate

MATERIALS
Empty glass bottles
Cloth measuring tape
Fabric crafting tape of your choice
Scissors

TIP Mix things up by cutting small dots from your fabric tape and using them to decorate the vase (**B**). Keep things consistent, or vary the size of the dots to really grab people's attention! Flowers, hearts, and stars would look great too.

TO MAKE THE VASES

1. Measure the length of your bottles, from the bottom to the beginning of the neck. Add 1 in. to this measurement, and cut 10 to 15 strips of tape (depending on how big your bottle is) to that length.

2. Remove the paper backing from one strip of tape and place it vertically on your bottle, where the neck ends and the bottle widens out. Tuck excess tape under the bottom of the bottle. Continue applying strips of tape to the bottle, overlapping slightly so that no glass is visible between the strips of tape.

3. Once the bottle has been covered on all sides with tape, measure the bottle's circumference where the neck ends and the bottle widens out. Cut a piece of tape in a complementary color or pattern to that length.

4. Remove the paper backing from the tape and wrap it horizontally around the bottle, smoothing into place as you go. This will cover the ends of the vertical strips.

A

B

Chevron Corkboard

Update your message board or just create a colorful wall hanging with this project, which turns corkboard squares into an eye-catching display. I used four, but you can create as many as you like.

SKILL LEVEL
Intermediate

MATERIALS
4 square corkboard wall tiles
Cloth measuring tape
Fabric crafting tape of your choice
Scissors

TO MAKE THE CORKBOARD

1. Begin with the upper left-hand corkboard tile. Measure diagonally from the center of the top edge to the bottom right-hand corner of the tile. Add 2 in. to this measurement; cut a strip of tape to that length.

2. Remove the paper backing from the tape and place the strip diagonally on the corkboard, moving from the center of the top edge to the bottom right-hand corner. Tuck the excess over the edges and secure it in back.

3. Repeat the process on the upper right-hand corkboard tile, inverting the angle of the tape so that it looks like a mirror image of the left-hand corkboard. When placed together, the tape strips on the two boards should create a V shape.

4. Repeat the process once again, with the lower left-hand corkboard tile. For this tile, place the strip diagonally from the top right-hand corner to the center of the tile's bottom edge. Again, repeat for the lower right-hand corkboard so that it mirrors the left. If done correctly, when the four boards are placed together the tape strips will make an X.

5. Place more strips of tape diagonally along the pattern to achieve a cool chevron look like mine or go crazy and create your own design!

Too-Cute Side Table

Use a combination of fabric and washi tapes to give an old table a colorful new face.

SKILL LEVEL
Beginner

MATERIALS
Small side table (unfinished wood or metal works best)
Fabric crafting tape of your choice
Washi tape of your choice
Scissors

TO MAKE THE SIDE TABLE

1. Starting at one corner of the table, cut a piece of fabric or washi tape long enough to cover the outer edge of the table. You don't want the tape to cover the sides of the table.

2. Working on a diagonal, continue cutting and placing strips of tape, overlapping them slightly so that the surface of table is completely covered.

Washi tape is somewhat transparent, so if you are covering a dark table, you'll be able to see it through the tape. To avoid this, simply place one to two more pieces of washi tape over the first one, until the table is no longer visible through the tape.

3. Once your tabletop has been completely covered, finish by measuring each edge and cutting a piece of tape for each. Remove the paper backing and place the tape so that it creates a border around the tabletop.

TIP Fabric tape edges may fray a bit, which adds a nice texture to your table. However, if you'd rather they stay clean, apply a thin layer of decoupage glue to the finished tabletop and allow it to dry completely before using.

B

A

Bedecked Bangles

Talk about arm candy! Plain wooden and metal bangles (**A**) are completely transformed with tape in this project, which takes almost no time to complete.

SKILL LEVEL
Beginner

MATERIALS
Fabric crafting tape of your choice
Scissors
Plain wooden or metal bangles

TO MAKE THE BANGLES

1. Cut a few 6-in. to 8-in. strips of fabric tape. Remove the paper backing from one strip and wind it around a bangle. Start by sticking the tape to the underside of the bangle and wrap at a slight diagonal. Overlap and smooth the tape as you go.

Resist the urge to cut one long strip of tape and attempt to wind it entirely around your bangle. You run the risk of getting the tape stuck on itself, creating unnecessary hassle.

2. When you run out of tape, start with a new strip. Always secure the tape ends to the underside of the bangle to give it a clean, seamless look.

VARIATION

If you have a bangle with a wider surface (**B**), try placing your tape flat down the center and along the sides for a bold look! Use pinking shears to add texture or lace tape for a fun vintage feel.

Heartfelt Tote

A basic canvas tote is transformed with a few strips of tape. I chose a heart shape, but anything—stars, flowers, and so on—would work just as well and come together just as easily.

SKILL LEVEL
Intermediate

MATERIALS
Wax paper
Clear tape
Fabric crafting tape of your choice
Scissors
Chalk
Plain canvas tote bag

TO MAKE THE TOTE

1. Tear a piece of wax paper large enough to accommodate your design and place it on a flat surface. Tape it down to keep it from slipping.

2. Cut pieces of fabric tape large enough to accommodate your design and begin sticking them on the wax paper, making sure there are no bumps. Overlap the strips slightly as you go, so that no wax paper is visible between them.

3. Once the wax paper is covered with enough tape to accommodate your design, use chalk to draw your design on the tape and cut it out.

4. Working carefully, peel the wax paper away from your tape pattern and then place the pattern on your tote. Smooth into place.

TIP To add an extra layer of texture to your heart shape, cut a few strips of fabric tape using pinking shears, which will give the edges a zigzagged pattern.

TIP For skinnier strips of tape, simply cut pieces of washi or fabric tape vertically in half. Try cutting it into thirds for even more slender strips.

Simply Striped Phone Case

Use a hard plastic case for this project and a variety of tapes in complementary colors. Stripes are a great graphic option, but any pattern will add a pop of color to every phone call.

SKILL LEVEL

Beginner

MATERIALS

Hard plastic phone case

Cloth measuring tape

Fabric crafting tape of your choice

Washi tape of your choice

Scissors

TO MAKE THE PHONE CASE

1. Measure the width of the phone case. Measure at a slight angle, as you will be placing the tape diagonally. Add 1 in. to that measurement and cut 7 to 8 strips of tape, depending on how much you'd like your case to be covered, to that length.

2. Place one strip of tape diagonally across the phone case, tucking the excess around the sides and securing it in back.

3. Continue in this way, placing strips of tape diagonally across the case, until it is covered to your liking. Make sure you don't cover the camera or input holes.

Well-Crafted Curtain

Fabric tape is a great way to add a colorful accent to a panel curtain and the pattern possibilities are endless. I chose a basic design, but think of your curtain as a blank canvas and let your imagination guide you!

SKILL LEVEL

Beginner

MATERIALS

Panel curtain

Cloth measuring tape

Chalk

Fabric crafting tape of your choice (you'll need at least three rolls; more if your curtain is very large)

Scissors

TO MAKE THE CURTAIN

1. Lay the curtain out on a flat surface. Using a measuring tape and chalk to measure and mark a few inches in and a few inches down from the top right-hand corner of the curtain. Repeat on all corners of the curtain.

2. Cut 2 lengths of tape the same size, each slightly longer (by about 2 in.) than the curtain's width. Cut 2 more lengths of tape the same size, each slightly longer (by about 2 in.) than the curtain's length. If your curtain is longer than a roll of tape,

simply cut 2 lengths and connect them by overlapping the tape slightly.

3. Remove the paper backing from the first length of tape and lay it widthwise across the top of the curtain, lining up the top edge of the tape with both chalk marks and folding the excess tape around curtain (to secure it in back). Repeat with the second length of tape along the bottom of the curtain.

4. Remove the paper backing from the third length of tape and lay it lengthwise down the left side of the curtain, lining up the left edge of the tape with both chalk marks and folding the excess tape around the curtain (to secure it in back). Repeat with the fourth length of tape down the right side of the curtain, lining up the right edge of the tape with both chalk marks.

> **TIP** Placing the tape in just the right spot is key for this craft, so don't go it alone. This is a great project to tackle with a friend!

Embellished Cardigan

This five-minute project totally transforms a simple sweater. One thing to remember: Fabric tape is not washable, so be sure to remove it before cleaning any embellished clothing.

SKILL LEVEL

Beginner

MATERIALS

Cardigan

Cloth measuring tape

Fabric crafting tape of your choice

Embroidery scissors

TO MAKE THE CARDIGAN

1. Measure the length of your cardigan, from collar to bottom hem. Add 2 in. to that measurement and then cut a strip of fabric tape to that length.

2. Remove the paper backing from the tape and place it on the front edge of cardigan (the side without buttons). Tuck the excess tape over the top and bottom of the cardigan, at the collar and hem.

3. Using the buttonholes on your cardigan as a guide, cut small slits in the tape strip with embroidery scissors so you can button the cardigan if desired.

TIP I used a single strip of tape, but you can make an even more colorful embellishment by using multiple strips, in different colors or patterns.

Sensational Sunnies and Sunglasses Case

Your favorite shades are even cooler with this tape treatment—especially when they come with a matching homemade case!

SKILL LEVEL
Intermediate

MATERIALS
Fabric crafting tape of your choice
Scissors
Sunglasses
¼ yard felt
Chalk

TO MAKE THE SUNGLASSES AND CASE

1. Cut a 5-in. to 6-in. strip of fabric tape, remove the paper backing, and wind it around one arm of the sunglasses. Repeat for the second arm.

2. Use the measuring tape and chalk to mark and measure a rectangle of felt that is 5 in. wide by 6½ in. long. Cut out the rectangle. This will be the body of the case.

3. Cut 6 to 8 strips of fabric tape that are 7 in. long. Remove the paper backing from the first strip and place it on the long edge of the felt rectangle, allowing about ½ in. of tape to hang off the long edge and ½ in. of tape to hang off one short edge.

4. Overlap the strips of tape slightly, until the entire rectangle is covered. When you are finished, both long edges and one short edge should each have a ½-in. overhang of tape.

5. Place one strip of tape perpendicular to the rest, along the remaining short edge, allowing ½ in. of tape to hang off top of edge. Fold the overhang over the felt and secure in place. This will be the opening of your glasses case.

6. To finish the case, fold the rectangle in half lengthwise, with the tape on the outside, sticking the ½-in. tape overhangs on both long edges together. Stick the bottom edge's overhang onto itself. Trim if needed.

Bead-azzling Jewelry

A variation on paper beads (often made from old magazines), this project (**A**) has limitless possibilities. Once you've mastered basic bead making, you can create necklaces, bracelets, key chains, and more.

SKILL LEVEL
Intermediate

MATERIALS
Fabric crafting tape of your choice
Scissors
Hollow plastic coffee stirrers
Embroidery needle
Embroidery thread

TO MAKE THE BEADS

1. Cut a 7-in. to 8-in. length of fabric tape. Use scissors to taper the length of the tape, so that you end up with a long, skinny triangle. Remove the paper backing and place the wide base of the triangle vertically on one end of a coffee stirrer. Wind the triangle of tape around itself on the stirrer, keeping it centered as you go.

2. Once the tape is completely wound around itself, cut the bead from the stirrer and set aside. Repeat Step 1 to make more beads; you'll need 25 to 30 beads to make a necklace and 10 to 15 for a bracelet.

3. Once you have enough beads to create the jewelry you want, thread the needle with embroidery thread and string the beads. Knot the thread to finish the necklace once all of the beads have been added. I finished my bracelet with a single barrel clasp: Just tie the thread onto the loop on the clasp for a more finished look.

Fabric Blooms

There are several different types of flowers you can make with fabric tape, but I love these elegant, unexpected calla lilies best. And unlike the real deal, they'll last you a lifetime!

SKILL LEVEL
Advanced

MATERIALS

Fabric crafting tape of your choice (the wider size works best here)
Scissors
Hollow plastic coffee stirrer
Floral wire
Wire cutters
Chalk
Drinking straw

TO MAKE THE FLOWER

1. Cut a 3-in. piece of yellow fabric tape into a long, skinny triangle shape. Place the wide base of the triangle on one end of the coffee stirrer and wind the triangle around itself, keeping it centered on the stirrer as you go.

Roll the tape as tightly as you can around the stirrer, avoiding gaps or looseness if possible. This ensures the center of your flower will retain its shape.

2. Once the tape is completely wound around itself, cut the wrapped tape section off of the stirrer and set aside. This is the center of your flower.

3. Cut four 4-in. lengths of fabric tape. Remove the paper backing and slightly overlap 2 pieces of tape, then repeat with remaining 2 lengths of tape. You should end up with two large squares of tape. Place them, sticky-side up, on your work surface.

4. Cut a 4-in. piece of floral wire and place it down the center of one of your fabric tape squares, so that it sticks in place. Place the second square, sticky-side down, on top of the wired square, so that the wire is sandwiched between the tape squares.

5. Use chalk to draw a calla lily (teardrop) shape on the tape square, making sure the wire is in the center of the shape. Cut out the shape.

6. Wrap the wider part of the teardrop around the drinking straw and use a piece of fabric tape to secure it at its base. Wind the piece of tape a few times around the straw to ensure the petal is securely in place.

7. Insert the yellow flower center inside the petal, securing in place with a small strip of tape. Gently bend tip of the flower petal backwards to create a calla lily shape.

Light up the Night

The prettiest way to keep things bright is with this embellished lampshade. Make sure you don't cover the top or bottom of the shade, which would trap heat and pose a fire hazard.

SKILL LEVEL
Intermediate

MATERIALS
Table lamp with lampshade
Cloth measuring tape
Fabric crafting tape of your choice
Scissors

TO MAKE THE LAMPSHADE

1. Measure the lampshade from top to bottom and add 2 in. to that length. Then measure the circumference of the shade. Use the circumference measurement to estimate how many strips of tape you'll need to cover the shade.

2. Remove the paper backing from the first tape strip and place it vertically on the shade, folding the edges over the top and bottom of the shade to secure in place.

Continue in this way, overlapping strips slightly as you go, so that the lampshade is completely covered by the tape.

3. Once the shade is completely covered, finish by cutting 2 strips of tape long enough to go around the top and bottom edges. Remove the paper backing and place the strips along the top and bottom edges, smoothing into place as you go.

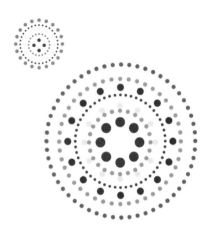

> **TIP** Keep your hues in mind when working on this project: Paler colors, like the yellow used here, will cast your room in soft, ambient lighting. Darker tapes may obscure too much light.

Patchwork Pillow

In this project (**A**), fabric tape gives simple throw pillows a crafty, quilted look, and lace tape adds an extra textural quality to them. Remember: The tape is not machine washable, so be sure to spot clean your pillowcases to preserve your design.

SKILL LEVEL
Beginner

MATERIALS
Solid-colored throw pillow

Cloth measuring tape

Chalk

Fabric crafting tape of your choice

Lace tape of your choice

Scissors

TO MAKE THE PILLOW

1. Using the measuring tape, determine where the center of the pillow lies. Mark this spot with chalk. Starting at the center of the pillow, place one 3-in.-square piece of tape. To really focus your design, use tape with an eye-catching pattern for this piece.

2. Cut strips of tape large enough to border this central piece of tape and place them on the pillow.

3. After applying the tape border, repeat a sequence of tape borders to get an interesting box-within-a-box effect. You can either keep things simple by using the same width of tape each time or vary your

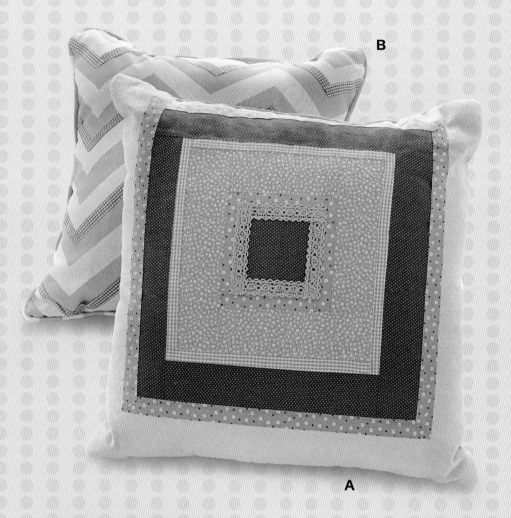

B

A

VARIATION
Have a patterned pillow? Dress it up by outlining the pattern with tape, as I did with this chevron design (**B**).

widths to get bands of alternating size. Make sure to overlap the tape edges slightly as you go, so that the pillow is entirely covered.

4. Finish with strips of lace tape outlining the center square.

B

A

Pretty Pockets

Even the simplest T-shirt looks a million times cuter with a little fabric tape (**A**). Remember, tape is not machine washable, so the pocket will need to be removed to launder the shirt.

SKILL LEVEL

Intermediate

MATERIALS

T-shirt with pocket

Cloth measuring tape

Fabric crafting tape of your choice

Scissors

TO MAKE THE POCKET

1. Use the measuring tape to determine the size of the pocket. Cut tape to fit. If the tape isn't wide enough to cover your pocket completely, simply cut 2 pieces of tape and overlap them to create the width you need.

2. Cover the pocket with tape, trimming as necessary to mimic its shape .

3. Finish the pocket by placing one piece of tape horizontally along the top edge, where the pocket opens, and trimming as necessary.

VARIATION To cover a sweatshirt's kangaroo pocket (**B**), place one fabric tape sheet on top of one side of the pocket and use chalk to roughly trace the shape of the pocket onto the fabric sheet. Repeat with a second fabric sheet on the other side of the pocket. Cut out the shapes, remove the paper backing, and place over each side of your pocket, trimming as necessary.

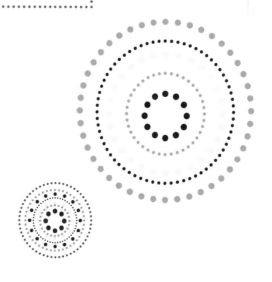

Colorful Candles

LED pillar candles are the perfect alternative to wax—you can place the tape directly on them without worrying about creating a fire hazard. Just don't forget the batteries!

SKILL LEVEL
Beginner

MATERIALS
LED pillar candles in graduated sizes
Cloth measuring tape
Fabric crafting tape of your choice
Washi crafting tape of your choice
Scissors

> **TIP** Try alternating colors or patterns with each strip to achieve stylish effects!

TO MAKE THE CANDLES

1. Measure the circumference of your candle set. Cut strips of fabric and washi tape about ¼ in. longer than the circumference of the candle. Starting at the top of the candle, remove the paper backing from one strip of tape and wrap it around the candle, making sure to do so evenly.

2. Starting at the same place as your previous strip, continue wrapping strips around the candle in the desired order.

3. Repeat the process with the remaining candles.

resources

DUCK BRAND DUCT TAPE
www.duckbrand.com

Duck Brand offers a wide variety of tapes to use on your craft projects, including a line of fabric crafting tapes that come in rolls and sheets, washi tapes, and the standard go-to—duct tape!

MAYA ROAD
www.mayaroad.typepad.com/ mayaroad

Maya Road's fabric and lace tapes are perfect for adding some interesting color and texture to your gear. They can be found online and at crafting stores.

WALMART®
www.walmart.com

Walmart carries all of the big brands of fabric and crafting tapes.

ETSY™
www.etsy.com

If you really want a style all your own, look on Etsy for custom tapes by home crafters.

CUTETAPE
www.cutetape.com

CuteTape is an online retailer specializing in crafting tape. They offer a great selection of washi, lace, fabric, and other tapes.

If you like these projects, you'll love these other fun craft booklets.

Arm Knitting
Linda Zemba Burhance
EAN: 9781627108867,
8½ × 10⅞, 32 pages,
Product #078045, $9.95 U.S.

Fashionista Arm Knitting
Linda Zemba Burhance,
EAN: 9781627109567,
8½ × 10⅞, 32 pages,
Product # 078050, $9.95 U.S.

Bungee Band Bracelets & More
Vera Vandenbosch,
EAN: 9781627108898,
8½ × 10⅞, 32 pages,
Product # 078048, $9.95 U.S.

Mini Macrame
Vera Vandenbosch,
EAN: 9781627109574,
8½ × 10⅞, 32 pages,
Product # 078049, $9.95 U.S.

DecoDen Bling
Alice Fisher,
EAN: 9781627108874,
8½ × 10⅞, 32 pages,
Product # 078046, $9.95 U.S.

DecoDen Desserts,
Cathie Filian and Steve Piacenza,
EAN: 9781627109703,
8½ × 10⅞, 32 pages,
Product # 078053, $9.95 U.S.

Tie–Dye & Bleach Paint
Charlotte Styles,
EAN: 9781627109895,
8½ × 10⅞, 32 pages,
Product # 078055, $9.95 U.S.

Rubber Band Charm Jewelry
Maggie Marron,
EAN: 9781627108881,
8½ × 10⅞, 32 pages,
Product # 078047, $9.95 U.S.

Beautiful Burlap
Alice Fisher,
EAN: 9781627109888,
8½ × 10⅞, 32 pages,
Product # 078054, $9.95 U.S.

Shop for these and other great craft books and booklets online: www.tauntonstore.com

Simply search by product number or call 800-888-8286, use code MX800126
Call Monday-Friday 9AM – 9PM EST and Saturday 9AM – 5PM EST.
International customers, call 203-702-2204